Poetry
That Will Speak
To Your Soul

Poetry That Will Speak To Your Soul

Lamar Hopson

authorHOUSE®

AuthorHouse™
1663 Liberty Drive
Bloomington, IN 47403
www.authorhouse.com
Phone: 1-800-839-8640

Published by AuthorHouse   04/20/2012

ISBN: 978-1-4685-8403-5 (sc)
ISBN: 978-1-4685-8402-8 (e)

Library of Congress Control Number: 2012907445

A Portrait of Sheba and Sonny

The different days when I met Sheba and Sonny it was love of a lifetime
Sheba was an innocent pup and Sonny was in his prime.
I first adopted Sonny from a crowded animal shelter nearby
Sonny is a handsome fellow but he seemed a little shy.
A year later I adopted Sheba so Sonny would have a mate
When I laid my tearing eyes upon her I didn't hesitate.
Sheba's hair is black as midnight and Sonny's a silky blond
When I take them for a walk or a ride my work is never done.
Sonny is such a gentleman and as well-mannered as he could be
My most shocking moment is when I saw Sheba watching the t.v.
I call them my kids because they plot to get on my nerves
Sonny will always surrender so all the attention is hers.
Sheba is very arrogant and she thinks she's all of that
Sometimes I'm done with both of them so I call them "Frick and Frat."
Sonny is getting on in years but he still knows how to act
Arthritis is in his bones but he won't renege on a fight.
Their ears are extraordinary long and they flip-flop when they walk
When they get out of hand I'll calm them down for a very long talk.
Sometimes I call Sonny, Buddha and sometimes I call Sheba, Boo
Therefore I'm dedicating this lovely portrait to the both of you.

Almost

Almost heard a whisper utter three sacred words ever so softly

Almost fell in love but became delusional over what was never meant to be.

Almost lend a hand but was scrutinized by society to only help the upper class

Almost saw forever but became permanently blind from forbidden sights from the past.

Almost cried a river while slowly drowning in emotional tears where peaceful water flows

Almost touched the sky but was disconnected from reality to connect to the one who knows.

Almost had a dream but became obsessed with fame and it came to an end

Almost lost the good fight to the words of the whisperer who lives within.

At Rest

Your journey is over but your life has just begun
Life won't begin until God's will be done.
Your journey was of a few days so those were His plans
We must never under-estimate the power of His hands.
For life here and now we must all stand the test
Where death shall be no more when we take our eternal rest.
Perhaps only time may control our loss
For your ship has sailed and you've made it across.
You're finally at rest where we all won't to go
Away from all the pain that you use to know.
Yes, your ship has landed and you're finally at rest
You'll be sadly missed for you were the best.

Being A Mother

Your son has no life and no place he can call his home
For your over protective tactics have caused his world to roam.
Your tears haven't helped they were a show to make him stay
You can stop your phony tears for your son has gone away.
You said that you tried to keep the peace but you created a war
Those ideas for making his decisions this time you went too far.
He has packed his belongings and left memories of things that use to be
Only if you had given him enough space and somewhere to run free.
Afraid to let him live a life that comes with making a few mistakes
Scared of a chance to fall in love because of the problems it creates.
The memories you left of being a mother can groom him to become a
good man
Even though you meant well, maybe he'll forgive you and one day he'll
understand.

Seldom Rest

We thought we understood you until that day you left and disappeared
For whatever choices you have made for your life we wouldn't have
    interfered.
We had our disagreements but we managed to savor some respect
We instilled in you to be considerate and we hope it took effect.
Something disturbing happen and it's still frightening until this day
Now our rarely talks are being ignored on why you ran away.
We felt cheated for we thought we knew you so well
You even lied to us and put us through a living hell.
Your father, a good man, who has always been there
Losing you to that cold world became his worst nightmare.
Your mother is heart-broken from all that you have put her through
She says that worrying comes easy but with life there's never a clue.
No matter what happens your happiness is our main concern
For our darling little girl we pray for a safe return.

Free At Last

A letter from my God today
I wonder what divine words He has to say.
O how unexpected and curious am I
He never sent me a letter and I never wondered why.

The letter said, "There is a time for us all and we all must go
I'm sending Death for you and I want to let you know."
My body felt frightened and my heartbeats were out of control
Old Satan cursed and laughed as he was trying to steal my soul.

Before I finished reading the letter, old Death walked in my room
I knew it was Death because I've heard about his awesome face of gloom.
I must have passed out of the thought that Death has come here for me
Little did I know or comprehend that I was dying to be free.

After I had revived, I ask Death, "Do I have to die?"
Death said, "Yes, God needs you so that's the reason why."
My mouth dropped open but I had to smile
When Death said, "You'll only be dead for a little while."

Death kept telling me how the streets are paved with gold
I felt mighty good all down in my soul.
Then I ask Death, "Will I ever see the end"
Death said, "No, but he was sure that I would never see him again."

I told Death that this way of dying it's so unique
When Death started reading the letter my body began to get weak.
Old Death knew it was time for me to go
Death said, "I'm taking you home and this you need to know."

I have heard of Death but I wondered why God sent him to me
Death heard my remark because I was nervous as I could be.
I was shocked and terrified with horror
When I heard Death read you won't be here tomorrow.

I listen to Death while I was praying on the ground
Suddenly, Death said, "Stop! You have won the crown."
I stood up saying, "Really, I haven't heard of such good news"
Then Death said, "When you live for Him you will never lose."

While I stood Death held me in the palm of his hand
It was old Death taking my soul to the Promise Land.
Death said, "Remember when I take you home you won't see me again"
So I had to shed a few tears for Death became my friend.

Well, I didn't fully understand what Death really meant
Death left me in my new home and back to earth he went.
Death has gone so I've taken the test and passed
I said to myself, "Thank God Almighty I'm free at last."

Go Ahead

Go ahead and show some love, because it's the right thing to do
Love will conquer all when your smile comes shining through.
Every day is not a bad day, so if you need a moment, go ahead
Just don't lose your faith when you feel you've been wrongfully misled.
Go ahead and give Him praise before your miracle comes your way
Don't let the green grass deceive you or put a damper on your day.
If you choose to give up and throw in the towel, go ahead
He will always love you, no matter what you've done or said.
Go ahead and put yesterday out of your troubled mind
Just be thankful for today and cherish the peace that you shall find.

He Knew

He knew about our heartaches for He gave us knees to pray
Even through our darkest night He has shown us a brighter day.
He knew there would be mistakes for He's always willing to forgive
Although we were dead but through His grace yet shall we live.
He knew about our sorrows and the tears they bring
For in His house are many mansions and a joy for everything.
He knew from the beginning about the trials we would face
Therefore He gave us faith to help us run this race.
He knew about our ups and downs and the peace we may never find
That's why He promised us eternal life if we would let our little light
    shine.

His Blood

The greatest love was when God gave His only begotten Son
That His blood cleanse our sins and His will be done.
He laid down His immortal life so that all could be free
Unselfishly, but willingly, He died on Calvary.
His blood paid for our debts so no fines do we owe
Just rejoice in His name and let the resentment go.
His blood reveals a beginning for those who believe in Him
With an eternal light that will never grow dim.
God gave His only begotten Son so that through Him we can receive
The greatest reward of everlasting life if we would only believe.

His Word

In the beginning God created the heaven and the earth and along came
    you and me
With a right to the tree of life and a claim to shout the victory.
For God so loved the world that He gave His only begotten Son
So put on the whole armor because sometimes this race gets hard to run.
Love ye one another but love Him with all your heart
His word is a bridge of faith that will never depart.
We all have sinned and come short of his glory today
We believe He died to wash our sins away.
Fret not thyself of wrong and evildoers for they will be cut down like grass
His word defines the meaning of forgiveness and true love that last.
Knock and the door will be opened and seek and ye shall find
His word transforms life in a new prospective and the past ways are left
    behind.
Weeping may endure for a night but joy cometh just before day
His word is everlasting and will never fade away.

Hopson/Clark Family Reunion Prayer 2004

O Father the Hopson/Clark family celebrates another time in unity and
praise

We just want to say thanks for guiding our family through the roughest days.

O Father as we celebrate the homecomings of our loved ones from down
through the years

Nothing but Your Amazing Grace and mercy we embrace with laughter
and tears.

O Father bless those who attended and those who couldn't for reasons
unknown

Please guide the Hopson/Clark family and let us know we're never alone.

O Father as we celebrate the culture and the roots of the Hopson/Clark
family

Just make us stronger and wiser, sharper and brighter as we bond in unity.

O Father when the celebrating is over and we must find our dwelling post

May our hearts leave with joy and an aching to hold You close.

Amen

Just To Say Thanks

Through my long and trying years, You've brought forth thy Amazing Grace
Just to say thanks for thy tender mercy that still remains in place.
Thanks for the gift of salvation and thy undying love has never strayed
Just to say thanks for thy wondrous miracles that always stand amazed.
During my trying years, You assured me that your words would never fail
Just to say thanks for the many blessings and the miracles as well.
Thanks for thy comforting words that encouraged me when I couldn't fall
    asleep
Just to say thanks for thy shield of protection and the promises You keep.
Thanks for being my rock when others wouldn't even dare
Just to say thanks for never leaving and giving thy extended care.
I can't say thanks enough with these glorious words of praise
Just to say thanks for bringing me from a mighty long ways.

Life Is Easier When You're Walking With The Lord

There are fewer sleepless nights, yet so many beautiful days
There are less heart-breaks just blessings in all different ways.
There are countless days of happiness where there was so much sadness
    and pain
There are numerous rays of hope where there's always sunshine after the
    rain.
The burdens have been lighter with less worries to employ
The sorrowing tears of self-pity are now my tears of joy.
The roads are smoother now so I fear less danger ahead
The dark clouds have passed to bring bright clouds instead.
The guilt trips are over and my conscience is finally free
This journey won't be easy but it's easier walking with Thee.
There were times my problems possessed me and I lived by their commands
Now my heart beats with ease for I put my life completely in His hands.
Now that my house is in order I can't lay down my shield and sword
For life is so much easier when you're walking with the Lord.

Life Is Like A Road

Life is like a road in which we all must plot
Making life worthwhile by being happy for what we got.
For life has its twist and turns with too many lefts and rights
Life is like a road with its bumpy rides and flashing caution lights.
With life we just live for who knows what's ahead?
For life is like a road that is frequently misread.
Life has its divided paths with a slew of turning lanes
Traveled by millions of people where survivors are their names.
Life is like a road and each must find their way
To face life as it comes day after day.

Old Nosey Lou

There once lived Old Nosey Lou
Who had to know it all because half wouldn't do.
She would peek from the curtains as cars drove by
I declare Old Nosy Lou could have been a private-eye.
She dipped here and dipped there
And I declare your business everywhere.
Old Nosey Lou was always on the phone
Eaves-dropping and gossiping as the news went on.
She always went to church and oh what a nose
She was always early so she could see who shows.
Everyone misses Old Nosey Lou
For delivering the news and the beef she use to stew.
Old Nosey Lou was murdered but some had reasons why
Some said, "She talked too much and God knows she had to die."

Over There

Over there must be a resting place
Away from the storms of life that we so often face.
The life He has given He's still in control
To ease our weeping sorrows that we can't behold.
We can't change yesterday and we can't live for tomorrow
All we have is today to wipe away the sorrow.
There must be a better life that is waiting for us all
We must prepare to be ready to hear the Master's call.
There is no easy way to handle our loss
God knows best and He's still the boss.
Life is not lived until God claims His own
Waiting for His children to sit around His throne.

Put Your Hands In God Hands

When trouble is knocking on your door
Even though you've said that you can take no more.
Why not put your hands in God hands
He rules the world and He hold all your plans?
Don't get all worked-up and feel so alone
God will work it out and for us to know how; it's unknown.
When you don't have money to buy food or pay your bills
Just remember what David did; he looked unto the hills.
Somehow God knows our sorrows and trouble each day
Always put your hands in God hands and He will make a way.
Don't give up the fight, no matter how heavy your load
God will grant you the strength to ease on down the road.
No matter what! Always put your hands in God hands
For He loves us all and our problems He understands.

Remembering Johnny

It's been over 10 years since you've been gone but your memories are still
with me today

Since you've been gone I learned that life is too short to let pride stand in
the way.

Over the years the tears have been from many too few and the pain about
the same

You're in that beautiful place where we'll meet again when He calls my
earthly name.

Every now and then I remember when we were kids and how we always
had a bond

Daddy and Kristie are with you in that place where your crying days are done.

Just searching through my memory I found that you were the greatest
brother and dad

I remember how you were so full of life and I remember all the good times
we've had.

Brother, you sleep on in God's beautiful garden because I won't let your
memories die

For as long as I can feel your presence I will never say good-bye.

Seldom Rest (The Reply)

I was a little embarrassed when you and dad filed a missing child report
I couldn't tell you what disturbingly happen but running away was my
    last resort.
You and dad raised me to be considerate and I've taken it all in stride
For the life of me I knew I had to tell you what I was keeping all inside.
Dad's best friend would come by frequently to sexual abuse your darling
    little girl
That's the reason why I was forced to run away and live in that cold, bitter
    world.
I've learned a lot about my life over the years from the streets where I hung
Someday I'll make a surprisingly return so you can sing your same old song.
Mom and dad I'm still overwhelmed about the way you said you care
Thanks for your concern but no thanks to the abuse while I was scared
    living there.
Dad I apologize for the nightmares because I know you love me and I
    don't have a doubt
I just couldn't live around your abusive friend so that led to my moving out.
To my poor mother, I'm so sorry and I know you're hurting inside
All the pain I've caused I know many nights you've silently cried.
No more tears mother you can wipe them all away
Your baby girl is coming home and she's coming home to stay.
So there's no need to be worried or concerned
I'm coming home to prove what in life I have learned.

You're Not Alone

I might can't make you smile but I sure can lend a shoulder
For you to come to cry on when your life grows older.
It really hurts when you're lonely and the pain is still sore
I might can't make you happy but you're welcome to my door.
For one reason or another we don't spread our love around
Yet, we're eager to criticize the ones who have stepped out-of-bound.
I might can't make you laugh but I'm sure going to give it a try
Because when I was down for the count you always stood by.
So many say, 'togetherness' but only a few have done
If we can only see that separation has no chance to bond.
I might can't make you listen, but one day it shall be
A lonely world divided between you and me.

The Memorial Service for Old Nosey Lou

It was another dark day when the town held the funeral for Sister Old
     Nosey Lou

Everyone in town was there to see if her sudden death was really true.

As they were viewing Sister Old Nosey Lou's body the preacher had yet
     to arrive

Someone said, "Sister Old Nosey Lou looks better dead than she ever did
     alive."

Some were there to say goodbye to a courageous woman who is gone
     forever more

It was when the choir was singing 'Soon and Very Soon' the tears began
     to pour.

Upon the preacher's arrival, he immediately spoke on behalf of Sister Old
     Nosey Lou

He said, "She was a dutiful church member but I can't say that about some
     of you.

Sister Old Nosey Lou gave her tithes and offerings to help the up-keep of
     this church

I'll miss Sister Old Nosey Lou as being a leader for our neighborhood
     search."

An old lady stood and said, "Sister Old Nosey Lou was sweet, but it was
     in her blood to pry

She even gave her mother's recipes to the same ones who wanted her to die."

A young lady said, "We should be thanking her instead of calling her the
     gossiper of the town

We're here today to give our condolences before we lay her in the
ground."

An old ex said, "I use to date Sister Old Nosey Lou when she was smoking
hot and young

But I had to cut her loose because her mouth couldn't hold back her
tongue."

When a seven year old stood up to speak there wasn't a dry eye in the place

He said, "Miss Old Nosey Lou, I love you but I never told you to your face.

Miss Old Nosey Lou you use to babysit me when I was left all alone

You gave me so much love and I'm sorry to see that you are gone."

At the cemetery, a court official issued summons to all who were standing
there

He even issued one to the preacher while he was gasping for some air.

When the memorial service was over, the preacher said, "There is one
thing we need to do

We need to figure out which one of us murdered Sister Old Nosey Lou."

The Murder Trial For Old Nosey Lou

The murder trial for Old Nosey Lou took place way back when
Everybody in town were suspects waiting for the trial to begin.
The judge ordered every suspect to please take the stand
Then he said, "If the truth ain't in you, don't raise your hand."
The first suspect said, "Old Nosey Lou was a sweet old lady may God rest
her soul
She should have been gone on a long time ago for all the lies she told."
Another suspect said, "Old Nosey Lou was a church going woman and she
didn't mean no harm
She just talked a little too much but I knew her day would come."
Another suspect said, "Old Nosey Lou was a busybody and she even tore
my marriage apart
She spread all kinds of rumors saying that my marriage was doomed
from the start."
Another suspect said, "Old Nosey Lou was murdered but whatever the
reason it was wrong
It was sad but Old Nosey Lou just dipped her nose where it didn't belong."
The last suspect said, "Old Nosey Lou told me to watch my back and said
my wife was no good"
She said, "Son, she's been slipping and sliding with the whole neighborhood."
We may never know who murdered Old Nosey Lou
Just don't let this current event to ever happen to you.

The Soul

I walked the long and narrow road all by myself because I had to and it
   was no one choice
but mine. In the late hours of compassion I prayed religiously for this old
   world that somehow
we would make it through. I had to search constantly trying to find my
   way and sometimes I
thought I would never stop. I didn't carry my heavy loads on my shoulder
   for I would cast them
in an old running river. I didn't engage in talking badly of others because
   I had to search deep
inside to see what was wrong with me. I didn't worry about what people
   thought and said
against me, besides what mattered was me. I tried to work out my problems
   and my
misunderstandings but when I totally failed I left them in a far better
   hand. I didn't dwell in
other people business for there was just enough time to run mine. I didn't
   give up when I didn't
succeed but I kept pushing forcibly for I knew soon I would find my way.
   I loved everyone
because I was told specifically to love you. Before things went terribly
   wrong in my life I kept a
little faith on hand so I would make it through. I tried to reach out to the
   ones who were lost
and I embraced those who were in desperate need of my help. I tried to
   understand instead of

criticizing and I gave willingly because His love was all I had. I prayed to
God to have mercy on

those who signed a petition for me to fall and I forgave those who closed
doors of opportunities

so I would lose my way on my long journey home. Before I chose to walk
the long and narrow

road I had to humble myself so I could let go and let God Almighty. I had
to be baptized,

immediately sanctified to qualify to walk the long and narrow road. While
I was walking the

long and narrow road I learned first-hand to take a little, but always give
your all from your

heart. I lived long enough to testify that there were times when I almost
gave up, but most of

my precious time I would kneel down to pray. While I was walking the
long and narrow road I

was faced with temptations, they were on call waiting to defeat me so I
would give up this race

on my long journey home. I soon realized they were my trials and
tribulations that were

questioning my vulnerability and the Creator of my strength. While I was
walking the long

and narrow road I made mistakes I even stumbled and fell along the way.
I had to stand-up

slowly so I can shake it off while I was freshly remembering my purpose
for walking the

long and narrow road. While I was walking the long and narrow road I
had to surround my

spiritual mind with positive thoughts so I would receive my life changing
experience through

the power of prayer. Before my journey was over, my spiritual mind
reflected on the many

people I met while I was walking the long and narrow road. My spiritual mind reflected on

how so many God-fearing Christians would take precious time and their abiding love too

often for granted. My spiritual mind also reflected on how so many Holy Ghost saints were

missing their blessings because they never learned how to forgive. As my spiritual mind was

reflecting on the past, it brought the memory of so many soldiers in the army of the Lord who

were walking around with hung down heads as though He hasn't risen so they would have a

key to one of His mansions if they would stay in His will. While my spiritual mind was still

reflecting I tearfully thought about how could I have walked the long and narrow road without

His Amazing Grace and how He restoreth my soul and leadeth me in the paths of righteousness.

All I wanted in that life was a world of perfect peace where we all could have lived together.

Before it was all said and done, there were dreams I prayed to see. Somewhere we can meet

again and another Soul to walk with me.

The Struggle

With the challengeable ordeals with life unknown
The burdens are plentiful, yet my faith presses on.
Every moment life is a battle between courage and fear
I strive for victory even when the signs of defeat appear.
Timing is crucial and with my every whim I mustn't give any slack
I'm waiting patiently but I'm prepared for whatever to attack.
It's a brutal fight to the finish line but only one can win
I'm determined to run this race to the weary end.
Someday this struggle will be over and this war shall be no more
I'm trusting in my faith to sail me safely to the other shore.

The Worriers

From dawn to dusk, and from noon to midnight
There live the Worriers whose burdens are never light.
Trouble waits at the door for the Worriers to receive
Only to worry more if trouble would ever leave.
Always restless with hearts at loose ends
The Worriers hearts and minds are not their best of friends.
The Worriers live in every big city and every small town
Worrying about people who never learned to turn their lives around.
The Worriers strive on living with stress; it's their daily routine
Worrying about their darken past from people they have never seen.
There's no peace for the Worriers for their hearts will always cry
Did I worry too much or not enough until the day they die.

This One's For You, Grandma

The abundance of love you gave is only a small part of your reward
The laughter you've shown us all when times got pretty hard.
It must be heavenly for God to find an angel so dear
Your presence is so missed but your memories are always near.
The chances you accomplished you left them all behind
Though the patience you endured brought you peace of mind.
You're in a place of rest where God only knows
You're in a class alone where He only chose.
I remember you were strong in your battles and wore a smile through the
     rough
I remember countless times you gave your all and you felt it wasn't enough.
The way you gave and earned respect that I'll never forget
I remember the trust you had in God with not one regret.
All may have forgotten but we must remember forever
The love you gave to this family that kept us all together.

Too Scared To Be Afraid

I can see the undying passion of hatred is burning like a wildfire that
   refuses to be
extinguished because I'm too scared to be afraid. I can feel the anguish lust
   of jealousy is
being memorialized for those who smiled and lied because I'm too scared
   to be afraid.
I can smell the arrogant fumes of racism thoroughly marinated with the
   bitter spices of
prejudice and handicapped by the ignorance that brought them fame
   because I'm too scared
to be afraid. I can see the influential youths have stopped marching toward
   a bright and
promising future when the band played 'There Will Never Be' because I'm
   too scared to be
afraid. I can see the guilty children are being rewarded with their freedom
   for numerous hits
and runs on those who made a change because I'm too scared to be afraid.
   I can feel the
elderly people have given up hope so they're searching for a safety net in
   the swamps of hell
for a decent place to rest because I'm too scared to be afraid. I can hear
   the wise voice of
reason slipping into a coma while shouting encouraging words to live by
   that no one wants

to hear because I'm too scared to be afraid. I can feel the chilly wind
  blowing gently in my

ear whispering a change will never come because I'm too scared to be
  afraid. I can see the long

and awaited tears streaming down wrinkled cheeks triggered by the
  everyday hell where there

is no heaven above because I'm too scared to be afraid. I can feel the Old
  South is quickly

returning to its traditional roots where the spacious plantations and the
  poplar trees have

never left because I'm too scared to be afraid. I can see that Lady Justice is
  no longer blind

so she's looking for the truth through rose-colored glasses while none but
  the righteous are

praising lily white lies because I'm too scared to be afraid. I can hear the
  butt-naked truth is

begging Lady Justice to run like the Jordan River because telling the truth,
  the whole truth, and

nothing but the truth, it won't set you free because I'm too scared to be
  afraid. I can see the

backstabbers and the hypocrites sitting together at the welcome table
  celebrating Communion

with clean hands because I'm too scared to be afraid. I can smell the sweet
  scent of success is

losing its fragrance after falling from a world of contentment to a world
  where two wrongs can

make a right because I'm too scared to be afraid. I can feel reality has been
  cancelled in order

to show never seen episodes of our skeletons in the closet because I'm too
  scared to be afraid.

I can see the storm clouds rising when the choir sings 'Nearer My God To
Thee' in a praising
kind of way because I'm too scared to be afraid. I can touch the cold hands
of Death only to
escape and to feel defeated by the cruelty of old Satan because I'm too
scared to be afraid.

Who's To Say?

Who's to say with life buts and ifs I can't live my dream?

Who's to say I gave up and became a victim to my low self-esteem?

Who's to say when the roads get rough I'll acknowledge fear to be my guide?

Who's to say love don't love nobody when my poor heart is breaking inside?

Who's to say I can learn from my mistakes when some people will never learn?

Who's to say life's just a gamble but I only lose when it's my turn?

Who's to say when the well runs dry all hell will break loose?

Who's to say I'll stand-up and fight or say, "What's the use?"

Who's to say when I fall I'll just lie there with no expectations to ever rise?

Who's to say I can't be successful and stay focused with my eyes on the prize?

Why Only At Christmas?

Why only at Christmas we make it a point to help the poor?
We do strange things at Christmas time that we never do before.
Why only at Christmas we lend a hand just to ease our guilt?
We block out the selfishness and the walls of hatred we once built.
Why only at Christmas our passionate hearts are at their best?
Giving and receiving the best of love is the homeless special request.
Why only at Christmas we look back through the year that has passed
Thinking of how we could have done more, but valued time never last?
Why only at Christmas our swollen hearts are filled with so much cheer?
We need to express our gift of love every day, not just one day out of the
    year.

With This One Chance

With this one chance to love my fellow man I got to give it all I've got
For all the reasons to believe that I can learn what love's about.
With this one chance to pray for forgiveness I must make every word clear
For Him to fully understand me by making my thoughts sincere.
With this one chance to be strong in this battle I got to fight until the end
It's my last chance to lose and my only chance to win.
With this one chance to redeem myself I must do it right away
For I must stay free from all doubts when I kneel down to pray.
With this one chance to make amends I must get in a hurry
There will be no chance for weakness so I need not to worry.
With this one chance to do what's right I must make haste
By devoting my time in praying with none to waste.

You're The One

You're the one who's holding you back from being all who you can be

You're the one who's looking in the mirror and saying that you don't like what you see.

You're the one who's deciding to throw sticks and stones as your new way to live

You're the one who's stressing out because you never took the test on how to forgive.

You're the one who's walking away when the road got hard and rough

You're the one who's raising your voice and saying that you've had more than enough.

You're the one who's complaining about how you have never gotten a fair shake

You're the one who's beating yourself up over what was just a simple mistake.

You're the one who's being left behind after you promised to do your very best

You're the one who's having a pity party for yourself while others could care less.

You're the one who's telling the world you're the man and real men don't cry

You're the one who's running from the truth after you told that bald-faced lie.

You're the one who's throwing a hissy fit because things are not going your way

You're the one who's opening your mouth to criticize but lately you have nothing to say.

You're the one who's pointing your finger at the ones who has gotten played

You're the one who's suffering the consequences from the bad choices you
    made.
You're the one who blamed others for your downfall that you created all
    by yourself
You're the one who should have fought for your dreams until you didn't
    have nothing left.
You're the one who can zoom in and out on your endless field of dreams
You're the one who has to say that your life is not as hopeless as it seems.

You Never Know

❦

You never know when you said, "I Love You" those words could have been your last

You never know about this thing called life, because time just moves so fast.

You never know when you will lose a loved one or when He'll call your name

You never know when your family will call and say that you're the one to blame.

You never know when the unpredictable storms in life will fill your eyes with tears

You never know when your friends will turn on you and one night can turn into years.

You never know when the doctors will say that you're running out of time

You never know when your burdens will be heavy and that mountain is hard to climb.

You never know when it will be your last hug or when the last time I'll see your face

You never know when your heart will stop or when someone will take your place.

You never know how much time you have to get ready for that eternal great beyond

You never know when your living days are over and when your crying days are done.

Easter

So many think of Easter as a wearing of something new
Some think of it as to attend church is the right thing to do.
As we gather here today I think about all He has done
First, He created the world and then He sacrificed His son.
Easter should remind us all of why we're here on this special day
No sad faces should we see just the reason to walk the narrow way.
I think of Easter of how He struggled to carry a cross to Calvary's hill.
To prepare a place for you and me to prove that His love is real.
Easter also reminds me of the holy blood he shed there
He paid the price of salvation and the burdens we bear.
Let Easter be a reminder to us for what He has done
He created the world and then He sacrificed His son.

The Three Women in My Life

Queen Esther, Ester Mae, and Brenda Gail you all are my one shining star
Without these three women in my life I wouldn't have made it this far.
Queen Esther, is my mother, therefore she has taught me right from wrong
I was a hard-headed child, but through her prayers my change came along.
My Queen is pure royalty with her humorous words when she would chat
Long live my Queen for she gave me life and I love her for that.
She's been there during my sickness and she has nourished me back to
    health
My reigning Queen is a remarkable woman of strength and I love her to
    death.
Ester Mae, is my oldest sister, who has a sweet heart with an unusual
    special touch
She will bend over backward for you and that's why I love her so very much.
Ester Mae has the gift of giving that she shares with so many others
She's a very special lady in my life and an inspiration to all loving mothers.
Brenda Gail, is my baby sister, who will display her love in a spontaneous way
She will give you her strongest hug if she feels that today was not your day.
Brenda Gail is an upbeat woman who chose forgiving to be her style
She's an optimistic kind of lady who loves for people to smile.
Without these three women in my life I don't know where I would be
I thank God for sending these three earthly angels to watch over me.

Any Job Can Be Fun

⚬━≈❦≈━⚬

Some have it easy and some can hardly bear it
But whatever, there's always a way to share it.
Lifting garbage cans day after day, some say can be fun
I guess after lifting a few, 'there's raisins in the sun.'
Digging holes to make water flow I've seen those workers sweat
A laugh at that if someone falls in and all their clothes get wet.
Arresting someone with an innocent face it seems like a life you can't lead
It makes you kind a smile when you know you're the person they need.
Booking a drunk driver or someone who committed a crime
The laugh may come later when they have paid their time.
Lunch is the best part of all when all are on their breaks
Thirty-minutes or an hour or how much time it takes.
But returning to serve their dreams to maintain a way
For a future of tomorrow and fulfillment of today.

Where Is That Place?

Where is that place where I can lay down my burdens and I can finally
 run free?

I got to find that place so I can greet my loved ones who have gone on
 before me.

Where is that place where I can receive my crown for walking this journey
 to the end?

There has to be a place where I can meet with Daniel so I can ask him
 about the lions den.

Where is that place where I can secretly escape to avoid life's unpredictable
 storms?

I must find that place so I can thank King David for writing those
 inspirational Psalms.

Where is that place where I can tell my story about all the trials that I've
 been through?

There has to be a place where I can just walk around with nothing else to
 do.

Where is that place where I will be judged by who I am and what I've
 accomplished on my way?

I got to find that place where there will be no signs of worrying to start
 my sunny day.

Where is that place where we won't have to live to sturdy war no more?

There has to be a place that is waiting for us way over on the other shore.

Where is that place where we can find happiness that comes with inner
 peace?

There has to be a place where love will conquer all and all heartaches will
 cease.

Where is that place where every day will be Sunday and the pastures are
    always green.
There has to be a place where we can find our creator whose face we have
    never seen.
Where is that place where we can meet again after this tiresome race is won?
There has to be a place where our crying days are over and our living days
    have just begun.

About the author

I started writing poetry when I was about twelve years old and I enjoy the thought that my poetry may inspire people with their everyday struggle in life. This poetry book is entitled, "Poetry That Will Speak To Your Soul" and I hope that it will be a great motivation for people that hope and believe prayers changes things in their everyday lives. Personally, these poetic words have brought me through many challenges in my life and I know there are people who can relate to these poetic words. My name is Lamar Hopson and I am from a small town named Donalsonville, Georgia. I graduated form Middleton Adult High School in Tampa, Florida. My mother name is Queen Esther Bell and she resides in Tampa, Florida. My father passed away in June, 2009. I am a country boy and I love to write from the bottom of my heart.